The Elephant's Trunk

Gina Cline
Robbie Byerly

This is an elephant.

Look at her trunk. She can do many things with her trunk.

The elephant's trunk is her hand, her arm, and her nose.

She smells with her trunk.
Elephants can smell
water from far away.

The elephant gets
water with her trunk.

She shoots water into her mouth. Her baby does, too.

The elephant uses her
trunk to take a bath.

She sucks up the water.
She spits water on her back.
She spits it on her ears, too.

The elephant uses her trunk to get food. Her trunk helps her get leaves from the tall trees.

Her trunk helps her
get the grass from
down on the ground.

The trunk brings the leaves
and the grass to her mouth.

She can mash the leaves
with her flat teeth.

She takes care of her
baby with her trunk.

When her baby is small,
the elephant can pick up
her baby with her trunk.

She walks with her baby.

The baby holds his mom's tail with his trunk.

The male lion wants
to eat her baby.

She blocks the lion from her baby. She flips up her trunk and makes a big sound. The lion goes away.

The elephant can do many
tricks with her trunk.

She plays with her trunk. Elephants love to play with their families. When it rains, they jump and crash in the mud.

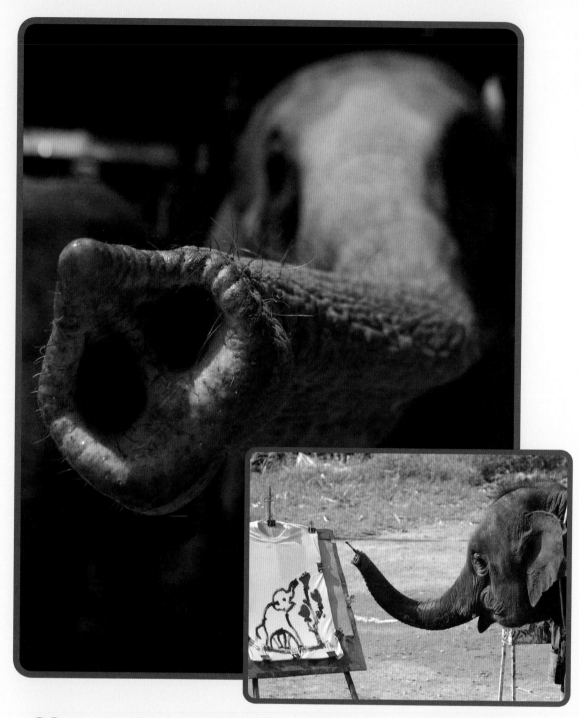

She can paint with her trunk.
She has this on the tip of
her trunk. This is how she
holds a paintbrush.

She can pick up trees with her trunk. She can hold over 600 pounds with her trunk.

She can hug people with her trunk. An elephant's trunk can grow up to 7 feet long. That could wrap around a lot of people.

She can pick up people with her trunk. She could hold three people on her trunk.

Use words you know to read new words!

it	all	and
sit	ball	band
spit	tall	sand
spits	small	hand

at
sat
rat
flat

Vowel Teams

out	see
spout	fee
pound	free
ground	feet

Powerful Word Families

You can use parts of these words to help you read LOTS of other words.

tip   clip   ship
rip   flip   whip

hug   slug   rug
bug   mug   jug

tail   mail   fail
rail   sail   jail

trunk   punk
skunk   sunk
clunk   chunk

Tricky Words

away	their
help	thing
long	use
people	walk